Dear Marion,
Thank you for an
unforgetable holiday '98.
Love you loads!
Lynn xxx & Mike x

DIANA

PORTRAIT OF A PRINCESS

With William and Harry at Highgrove, August 1988

DIANA
PORTRAIT OF A PRINCESS

by Jayne Fincher, Royal Photographer

Text by Jayne Fincher with Judy Wade

CALLAWAY

EVERGREEN

State Opening of Parliament, London, November 1982

To the memory of Diana

CONTENTS

PREFACE

*Buckingham Palace,
June 1990*

*Prince Edward and me,
July 1987*

Not many photographers can claim to have had Diana, Princess of Wales, as an assistant on a photo shoot. She happily helped me set up my lights and crawled around the floor connecting electric plugs when I was invited to do a private session on Prince Charles's 40th birthday.

For 20 years I have spent almost more time with the royal family than with my own. As soon as Diana came on the scene in 1980, we became friendly since I was the only woman among the crowd of cameramen who regularly covered the world's most famous family. It has been a challenging job, and the competition tough. On only a few occasions has being female been an advantage.

On one assignment in Nigeria with Charles and Diana, the Princess went to visit with the women in the harem at the Shehu's palace in Maiduguri. According to local custom, only women are allowed inside, so, to the annoyance of my male colleagues, I swept through the door with Diana and got the only photographs.

In the Gulf States, men and women are rigorously separated at social functions, but when the Princess arrived she was given a special dispensation to attend some events that are normally a male preserve. Reporter Judy Wade, Diana's female staff, and I were permitted to watch the camel races in Riyadh,

Australia, March 1983

where everyone else at the track was male. We were also invited to King Fahd's palace for a grand dinner, although we women, including Diana, were allowed to attend only the pre-dinner reception and could not sit down to eat with the men.

One of the main disadvantages of this job is the sheer physical stamina needed. Heavy camera equipment, computers, and that vital asset, an aluminum stepladder, have to be carried everywhere. My small steps have traveled the world with me, much to the amusement of the airline check-in staff. I suspect they think I am a wandering window cleaner. Usually, I explain that members of the royal family are surrounded by security men, officials, and the general public waving flags, so I need some elevation to get a clear view of my subject. But it can be tricky to balance in deep snow or soft desert sand.

I have suffered altitude sickness on the dizzy heights of the Tibetan Plateau, broken my leg on the slopes of the Swiss ski resort Klosters, been bowled over by heat exhaustion in Egypt's Valley of the Kings, and camped in the cholera unit of an African refugee camp, all in a bid to get a great picture.

*The press awaits the honeymooners,
Balmoral, August 1981*

I often compare the job with being a footballer. You have glorious periods when the goals keep on coming with one good photograph after another. Then there are days when you expend a lot of time and effort but go home without scoring.

Roughly 90 percent of a news photographer's time is spent waiting and planning to cover an event

Photographing Diana, Cardiff, Wales, November 1983

that often lasts only a few minutes. Endless backaching hours perched on a ladder are devoted to gaining just one split-second on film.

I was lucky enough to have had several private photo sessions with Diana and her family. One was a special session at the Prince and Princess of Wales's country home, Highgrove, in 1988. This was a nerve-wracking day for me because I had been asked to take the official photographs for Prince Charles's 40th birthday. I arrived feeling as if I were about to have all my teeth extracted without anesthetic, but my nerves soon vanished in the warm atmosphere of the Waleses' home. William and Harry were delightful youngsters, not spoiled little royal princes. Just like other children, they did not like sitting still for photographs. But as Charles and Diana gently coaxed them to face the camera, it was apparent just how close they all were.

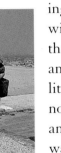

Judy Wade and me, Egypt, May 1992

There have been many other exciting occasions in my royal career. I have sipped tea with Queen Noor of Jordan at her home overlooking the Red Sea in Aqaba, enjoyed a personal guided tour of Buckingham Palace given by Prince Edward, and helped William and Harry groom their ponies in the stables at Highgrove.

Over the years I have had the great privilege of meeting kings and queens, world leaders, celebrities, and even the pope. In 1985 the Prince of Wales himself introduced me to Pope John Paul II after a royal audience at the Vatican. It came as a total surprise, and all I can remember is that I didn't know whether to kiss his hand or curtsy.

All the photographs I take are authorized by the palace, but in recent years there has been a growing demand for the informal, often intrusive, photographs taken by the paparazzi. Some curbs have been imposed on their alarming activities since the Princess's death, but I became so disturbed by their pursuit of Diana in the last year of her life that I almost quit.

In my hotel room with equipment, Gambia, Africa, February 1990

I felt great empathy for her. From the start, we got along very well, working with what I think of as a mutual respect.

I often felt that when she gazed into my camera lens her look was different from the ones she directed at my male colleagues. While she gave them a

The press outside St. Mary's Hospital after Harry's birth, London, September 1984

flirty, sometimes sultry glance, her expression was more relaxed and vulnerable with me.

The saddest assignment of all for me was, of course, covering her funeral. I never want to go through a day like that again. I look back and wonder how I managed to focus my lens through my tears. People may well ask why I agreed to cover the funeral. I can only explain that it was a way of saying goodbye in the way I know best – my professional capacity. I had recorded all the other major events in Diana's life: The excitement leading up to her wedding, the birth of her babies, and her trips around the world. How could I miss recording her last journey?

People always ask what my most lasting memory is of the Princess. She had so many facets. Diana was not always as angelic as most of her admirers seem to think and could, at times, be extremely difficult to work with. She was human like the rest of us. Of course, she was also compassionate and kind, eternally elegant and enthusiastic. But I remember best that she was fun. Diana loved gossiping and giggling with me about the guys we worked with.

And then there was her unforgettable charm and immense physical beauty. When she walked into a room, every man was mesmerized and every woman envious. My male colleagues always called her Blue Eyes and that's my most vivid memory of her – those enormous cornflower-blue eyes. I miss her.

Waiting on the runway at Aqaba airport, Jordan, March 1984

9

MY FIRST ENCOUNTER

On a cold November night in 1980 I was standing shivering outside the Ritz Hotel in London. The Queen's sister, Princess Margaret, was celebrating her 50th birthday, and I was waiting with several other press photographers for the royal guests to arrive.

Suddenly I felt a tap on my shoulder and turned to see a young blonde who politely asked if we would let her through. As she walked into the hotel one of my colleagues said, "I'm sure that's Lady Diana Spencer – you know, she's the girl they say is Prince Charles's new girlfriend."

As I stared at her disappearing figure wrapped up in a heavy overcoat, I simply could not believe it. She seemed such an unlikely candidate to become the Prince's new love.

She looked very young (I later learned she was only 19) and had short, boyish bobbed hair. Her round, rather plump face was almost bare of makeup and her clothes were far from stylish. Her dark green wool Loden coat covered a fussy pink-and-gold evening dress. On her feet she wore flat gold ballet pumps.

In more than ten years of photographing the royal family I had seen many of the young women who became known as Charlie's Darlings. They had all been worldly blondes around the same age as the Prince, who was then 32. This new girl was distinctly different. She was not only much younger than the Prince of Wales but seemed too demure and rather too dowdy to catch his eye.

Lady Diana Spencer had first been spotted with Charles on a riverbank at Balmoral, in Scotland, two months earlier. She was staying at the royal family's Highland home with her older sister, Lady Jane Fellowes, the wife of the Queen's private secretary, Sir Robert Fellowes. Jane had just given birth to a baby girl, and Diana, who adored little children, was invited to help the tired new mother.

But Balmoral estate workers noticed that she spent less time on baby care and more with the lonely prince. She followed him around "like a little lamb" one Scottish ghillie revealed.

When Diana returned to London she became front-page news with reporters and cameramen following every move she made. As I waited for the guests to leave the Ritz, I decided that I should take another look at the girl who was suddenly hitting the headlines. She finally emerged from the hotel in the early hours of the morning and was hurrying down the street to her car when she saw my camera. As I snatched a few quick shots, she blushed and pulled her coat up around her face.

I could never have believed then that this shy girl would soon be transformed into a dazzling fashion icon and those first few frames would be the start of thousands of photographs I would take over the next 17 years of the world's favorite princess.

THE ROYAL HUNT

SEPTEMBER 1980 – FEBRUARY 1981

From the time her royal romance was revealed in September 1980, Diana lived virtually under siege from the media. Going to work at the Young England kindergarten became a daily ordeal for the Princess-to-be, who had no police protection at the time. Although secretly panicky and frightened, Diana kept smiling and often outwitted her pursuers. Prince Charles and his family were quite impressed with the way she coped.

Left: Diana's first-floor apartment at Coleherne Court, South Kensington, soon becomes every photographer's favorite target. London, November 1980

FOR LOVE

1980–1984

Top row, left to right: Broadlands, Hampshire, March 1981; Tetbury, Gloucestershire, May 1981; Wedding day, Buckingham Palace, London, July 29, 1981; Aintree, Liverpool, April 1982
Middle row, left to right: Guards Polo Club, Windsor, May 1982; St. Mary's Hospital with Prince William, London, June 1982; Braemar Games, Scotland, September 1982; Newcastle, Australia, April 1983
Bottom row, left to right: Aberdeen airport with Prince William, Scotland, October 1983; Wentworth Hotel, Sydney, Australia, April 1983; Kensington Palace with Prince William, London, December 1983;
St. Mary's Hospital with Prince Harry, London, September 1984

THE DEBUT OF DIANA

The perfect blend of regal and real, Lady Diana Spencer was the answer to a nation's prayers, not to mention those of photographers like myself, when she first appeared in September 1980. She was a genuine English rose with blond hair, blue eyes, and a peachy complexion. But great looks were only part of her appeal. This aristocratic young lady was the daughter of an earl and a descendant of both Henry VII and James I. She was also seemingly self-possessed, with a quick-fire supply of quips. Inevitably, she stood out like an Afghan hound among corgis beside the women of the House of Windsor.

The British public and the press immediately fell in love with her, convinced that Diana was not just deliciously pretty but also had all the qualities to be a queen. She was the right girl for Britain, we decided, never asking if she was the right girl for Charles.

A closer look at this demure country girl might have caused concern. Diana had an unstable background and, at 19, felt she had no real home. Her mother, Frances, left her husband after years of unhappiness when Diana was six. Frances remarried wallpaper heir Peter Shand Kydd and had only limited contact with her four children.

Left and right: Diana wows her future neighbors on her first visit to Tetbury, the town nearest to Charles's country home, Highgrove, in Gloucestershire. May 1981

Although Diana's relationship with her father, Earl Spencer, was warm and close, she did not like his second wife, Raine, whom she dubbed Acid Raine, and felt unwelcome at the Spencer stately home, Althorp, in Northamptonshire. Her much-adored elder sister Sarah had suffered for years from the eating disorder anorexia nervosa and had briefly been involved with Prince Charles, who continued to give her a great deal of support.

The first time Charles and Diana could recall meeting each other was in November 1977, when the Prince joined a shooting party at Althorp as Sarah's boyfriend. Diana, then 16, was introduced to him in the middle of a plowed field near Nobottle Wood on the Spencer estate. Over the next three years their paths would cross more often. Diana was just one of a number of attractive girls invited to parties at royal palaces and house parties on the Queen's estates. Charles began to enjoy her company more and more.

In September 1980 she was first spotted by the press on a riverbank at Balmoral watching the Prince fishing in the River Dee. Noticing journalists emerging from the bushes on the other side of the river, she quickly displayed a talent for media manipulation that was to become an art form in the years ahead. Hiding behind a tree, she whipped out a powder compact from her pocket and slyly watched the pressmen in its mirror.

No one got a clear picture of the future Princess that day. Right from the start, Diana was proving to be a challenge. Then, back in London, the girl who had outsmarted Britain's top photographers suddenly became more cooperative. She smiled coyly at reporters and said, "You know I can't talk about the Prince or my feelings for him." It was a sentence packed with implied meaning. So she did have feelings for Prince Charles!

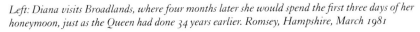

Left: Diana visits Broadlands, where four months later she would spend the first three days of her honeymoon, just as the Queen had done 34 years earlier. Romsey, Hampshire, March 1981

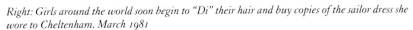

Right: Girls around the world soon begin to "Di" their hair and buy copies of the sailor dress she wore to Cheltenham. March 1981

Lady Diana Spencer attends her first film premiere, for For
Your Eyes Only *at Leicester Square, London, June 1981*

This was the beginning of Diana's long love-hate relationship with the press. Although outwardly polite and smiling, she was constantly planning how to evade us with decoy cars parked outside her home while she skipped out back and drove off in taxis.

From the outset there was no doubt that Diana wanted to save the Wales from his lonely bachelor life. She hoped to outmaneuver all the worldly blondes who had loved and lost the world's most eligible man. She once told a school pal, "I'd like to be a ballerina, or maybe Princess of Wales."

Diana grew too tall to become a ballet star, and having flunked out of school, she had no real qualifications to embark on a serious career when she moved to London. She experimented with a number of part-time jobs, including housecleaning, baby-sitting, and teaching children in a dancing school. Eventually, she began working as an assistant at the Young England kindergarten in Pimlico. She left most of these jobs after only a short time as she aimlessly tried to find something interesting to do. A good marriage seemed to be the answer to her problem.

Above and right: Diana proved on her very first official evening engagement with Charles that she would be dazzlingly different from other royal ladies. When they arrived, a proud Prince Charles told us, "You won't believe what's coming next!" And as Diana bent low to step out of their car, she almost fell out of the top of her stunning gown. There was no doubt that the girl believed to be so shy and demure could be incredibly alluring. One newspaperman quipped, "As coming out parties go, Lady Diana could hardly have come out any further." Goldsmith's Hall, London, March 1981

Many people closely connected to the royal family privately doubted that the union between the charming but immature Lady Diana Spencer and the sophisticated, solemn Prince would work out. She was a very young 19, while Charles was a very mature 32. In addition to this yawning 12-and-a-half-year age gap, they seemed to have little in common.

He was a history graduate who enjoyed opera, art galleries, and the company of deep thinkers. She was more keen on shopping and bopping to pop music. Nothing more weighty than a charge account at Harrods seemed ever to have crossed her mind.

But the world wanted to notice only the links between the lovers. Her father was a former royal equerry whose family had served Charles's for centuries. She was literally the girl next door, who had grown up at Park House, next door to the Queen's Norfolk home, Sandringham House.

Well-meaning people assumed that Diana's troubled family history had given her a resilience that would steer her through the difficult adjustment from naive nobody to gorgeous royal bride. Sadly, the opposite was true.

Diana had the blessing of the British. She also had a steely determination to get her man. She was absolutely sure that she wanted to marry Charles. Her teenage dream of capturing the heart of a prince was coming true. When people pointed out the loneliness, the lack of privacy, and other problems of life at court, she never wavered. "It's what I want," she said. ⬦

Above and left: Only four days before her wedding, Diana looks nervous during a polo match at the Guards Polo Club. A crowd of several thousand had shown up to see the future Princess. Windsor, July 1981

A camera-shy Lady Diana Spencer at the Guards Polo Club, Windsor, June 1981

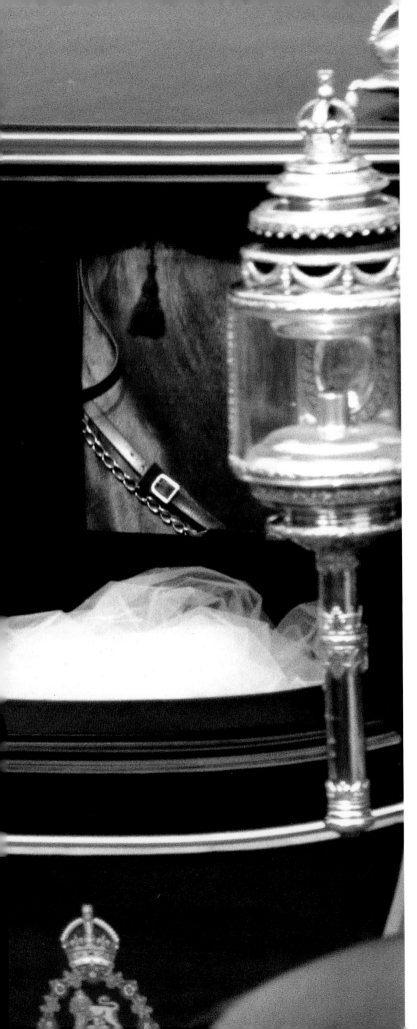

Prince Charles rides to St. Paul's Cathedral with his best man, Prince Andrew. London, July 29, 1981

THE WEDDING

JULY 29, 1981

"This is the stuff of which fairy tales are made," said the Archbishop of Canterbury when he blessed the union of Charles Philip Arthur George, Prince of Wales, and the Lady Diana Spencer. In the hour-long ceremony the former nursery assistant became the Princess of Wales, future Queen of England, Scotland, Wales, and Northern Ireland.

The nervous bride hadn't slept a wink all night, and the groom had been up from the early hours, listening to the crowds singing outside Buckingham Palace. "It really was remarkable," Charles recalled later. "I found myself standing in the window with tears pouring down my face."

Critics later claimed that Charles had never really loved his wife, but in the weeks before their wedding, I had my camera focused on the couple constantly, and they certainly convinced me they were head over heels in love.

On the big day, I had a prime position outside St. Paul's Cathedral and enjoyed watching the guests, from humble royal estate workers to America's First Lady, Nancy Reagan, arriving with members of the royal family. We all held our breath when the beautiful bride stepped from her coach, and for a moment there was stunned silence. "Oh, her dress is all creased," came a cry from the crowd. It was true! Diana's vast crinoline skirt of ivory silk and old lace had been squashed in the long procession from Clarence House to the church, and it took some time for her bridesmaids to rearrange her 25-foot train.

Lady Diana and her father, Earl Spencer, travel in the glass coach to St. Paul's Cathedral. London, July 1981

When she reached the altar, her misty-eyed groom took her hand and said, "You look wonderful." Diana gazed into his eyes dreamily. "Wonderful for you," she whispered.

Was it an omen when both the bride and the groom made gaffes during the ceremony? She mixed up her husband's name and promised to love, honor, and cherish "Philip Charles Arthur George." Prince Andrew laughed, "She's married my father!" Charles appeared stingy when he vowed to share all Diana's worldly goods instead of his own, saying, "And all thy goods with thee I share."

Fanfares heralded their walk back down the aisle as man and wife, then they stepped out through the west door of St. Paul's into the sunshine as bells pealed and thousands cheered.

The wedding ceremony, St. Paul's Cathedral, London, July 1981

The bride arrives at St. Paul's Cathedral. Lady Diana's 25-foot train draws gasps from the crowds as she climbs the steps. London, July 1981

Above, right, and overleaf: The royal wedding carriage procession heads down Ludgate Hill away from St. Paul's Cathedral after the ceremony. London, July 1981

The Prince and Princess of Wales in a 1902 State Landau, London, July 1981

The bride and groom on the steps of St. Paul's Cathedral after the ceremony, London, July 1981

The balcony at Buckingham Palace, London, July 1981

The Princess, surrounded by her pages and bridesmaids, looks so happy as she gives a final glance to the crowds outside Buckingham Palace. July 1981

The Honeymoon

August 1981

Gibraltar

A dazzling sea of cheering faces, waving hands, and clicking cameras greeted Charles and Diana when they flew to Gibraltar to begin their honeymoon cruise through the Mediterranean.

The royal couple touched down in an antiquated twin-propellered Andover of the Queen's Flight, piloted by the Prince. The first three days after their wedding had been spent in the peace and seclusion of Broadlands, the Hampshire home of Prince Charles's Mountbatten cousin and best friend Lord Romsey. This break from the spotlight had left Diana more relaxed than we had seen her for weeks, although she still seemed shy as she clung to her husband's arm.

Charles gently guided his bride up the long red carpet covering the gangplank onto the yacht. Following royal custom, they were piped aboard, then stood on deck whispering and giggling to each other. They held hands and looked so happy as they gazed out at the late afternoon sunlight dancing on the water. Diana seemed overwhelmed by it all, a local official who greeted them told me later. She kept gazing at the scene around her and brushed away tears. She stayed close to Charles, never letting go of his hand, and it was wonderful to see two people so in love.

Gibraltar, August 1981

Above and right: Arriving at the Royal Air Force base airport after their honeymoon cruise, Lossiemouth, Scotland, August 1981

THE HONEYMOON

AUGUST 1981

BALMORAL CASTLE

Diana and Charles were delighted that not one photographer caught up with them until the end of their cruise. In a bid to compensate us for a wasted journey, the following week they agreed to a photo call at Balmoral Castle, where they had begun the second stage of their honeymoon. Prince Charles chose a very scenic location among the heather on the banks of the River Dee near an old stone bridge.

The deeply suntanned couple strolled along the riverbank towards us holding hands and laughing together. When they paused to face the cameras, Diana rested her head on her husband's shoulder and giggled when asked how she was enjoying married life. "I can highly recommend it," she said with that famous coy smile.

More than 50 cameramen had gathered to capture this happy scene on film and had clubbed together to buy a bouquet of flowers to present to the Princess. When a reporter handed them over, Diana gave him a teasing smile and quipped, "I suppose these came out of your expenses."

These pages: Set in the picturesque heather-clad mountains near Balmoral Castle, the Braemar Highland Games has become an annual event for the Queen and her family. The Prince and Princess accompanied the Queen to the games during their honeymoon. During the games, I saw Diana gaze often into her new husband's eyes. Scotland, September 1981

WALES WELCOMES ITS PRINCESS

NOVEMBER 1981

The Prince and Princess at Caernarvon Castle, where Charles was invested as the Prince of Wales at the age of 21 in 1969.

Diana's real initiation into royal life came in November 1981 on her very first tour, an exhausting three-day trip to Wales, in which she and Charles covered 400 miles and every county in the principality. They endured threats of violence, constant rain, and outbreaks of Di-mania when crowds made it clear they had come to see their Princess, not her husband. To please her new people, Diana dressed patriotically in the red and green colors of the Welsh flag and delivered her first public speech, declaring, "How proud I am to be Princess of such a wonderful place and of the Welsh who are very special to me." And to the delight of the thousands who had welcomed her to their country, she added in their language, "I hope to come here again soon."

FIRST AND WORST MONTHS

Diana was so thrilled to be pregnant within two months of her marriage that she wore voluminous maternity clothes from the day her happy event was announced. Fashion editors raved about the way her ruffled necklines drew attention away from her blossoming bump. However, constant morning sickness forced her to cancel many engagements, declaring, "No one told me I would feel like this." During a visit to the north of England in which she carried out three walkabouts in a single day, she told a well-wisher, "I haven't felt well since day one. I don't think I'm made for the production line."

The Princess arrives at the Victoria and Albert Museum for an evening gala recital. Already pregnant, though this was not yet public knowledge, she looked thin and pale. London, November 1981

The day her pregnancy was announced, Guildhall, London, November 1981

Barbican Concert Hall, London, March 1982

Christmas Day, Windsor Castle, December 1981

Scilly Isles, Scotland, April 1982

Only days before the birth of William, Diana looks fed up and tired.
Guards Polo Club, Windsor, June 1982

Brigend, Wales, April 1982

Guards Polo Club, Windsor, May 1982

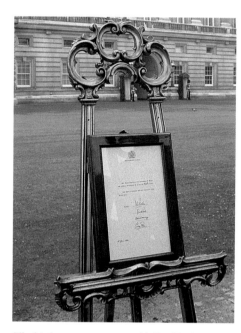

The birth announcement outside Buckingham Palace, London, June 1982

Left and right: St. Mary's Hospital, London, June 21, 1982

WILLIAM'S BIRTH

JUNE 21, 1982

A gun salute for the new heir, Hyde Park, London, June 1982

In August 1988, when I met Diana for a private photo session, she asked me, "Do you remember how I smiled when I walked out of the hospital carrying William? Actually, I was in agony! I could barely walk, and as soon as we got into the car and drove away, I collapsed in tears. It was just too much, facing photographers less than 24 hours after my baby had been born. I had a real attack of the baby blues and sobbed all the way home to Kensington Palace."

Princess under Pressure

By October 1982, Diana was in the grip of postnatal depression and steadily losing weight. Public concern was expressed that she might be anorexic after she appeared with protruding shoulder blades and painfully thin arms at a Guildhall fashion show in London the following month. The switch from unknown London working girl to royal fiancée, bride of the century, then mother, all within one year, sent Diana's stress levels way past the danger point. She was a princess under pressure, although not even those of us who saw her almost every day realized the seriousness of her plight. In private she was bingeing on junk food, then making herself sick.

The Princess attends a gala concert at St. David's Hall. After the concert she did a walkabout in the dark street outside the concert hall, an unusual act for a royal in an evening gown. Cardiff, Wales, October 1982

Barbican Concert Hall, London, October 1982

Guildhall, London, November 1982

The Princess always drew a large crowd of cameramen
when she attended events such as a film premiere. Here
she is arriving for the premiere of E.T. It was during
this period that the Princess was looking very thin and
stories were appearing about possible anorexia.
Leicester Square, London, December 1982

A PLEA FOR PRIVACY

NOVEMBER 1982

At first the Queen sympathized with Diana's struggle to adjust to her strange new life. "She is not like the rest of us," Elizabeth explained to her family when the new Princess's tears and tantrums astonished her in-laws. "She wasn't born into our way of life." So concerned did the Queen become that she called Fleet Street editors together in an unprecedented plea to give her son's wife more privacy. The Queen also procured help for Diana from psychiatrists. State Opening of Parliament, London, November 1982

ON THE SLIPPERY SLOPES

JANUARY 1983

On her first skiing holiday with Charles, Diana began to cry when they were trapped by cameramen in an alleyway. As the photographers blazed away, she lowered her head into the collar of her ski suit and began shrieking, "I can't stand it. I can't stand it!" Charles rapidly lost his cool, and I heard him say, "Please, darling, don't be stupid." Luckily, their car turned up at that moment and whisked them both back to the castle in Vaduz, where they were staying. Lech, Austria, January 1983

DIANA DOWN UNDER

MARCH – APRIL 1983

Walking up Parliament Hill, Canberra, Australia, April 1983

In March 1983 Diana embarked with Charles on a six-week slog around Australia and New Zealand. It was a punishing ordeal for a royal novice, but the Princess came smiling through floods, bushfires, and droughts as they toured Australia from the sunbaked Outback to the cities by the sea. Their schedule was grueling, with more than 40 flights from one state to another to shake thousands of hands on an endless round of banquets, civic receptions, and walkabouts among the public.

The crowds were friendly to the Prince, but they were wild about his wife. In Brisbane, Queensland, 400,000 people turned out to see the new Princess, bringing the city center to a standstill. The warmth of their welcome temporarily banished Diana's depression. She gained confidence as Charles guided her through their ceremonial duties. I saw him whispering instructions as they laid a wreath at Canberra's Cenotaph, and he held her hand to give her reassurance when she needed it. Di-mania erupted everywhere they went on the 45,000-mile tour, and Charles soon realized that Diana was now the star attraction. When they walked down opposite sides of a street, the disappointed crowds who got him openly groaned. It was a rude awakening for the Prince, but he good-naturedly commented, "I'm sorry. I've only got one wife – and she's over there!"

Sydney Opera House, Australia, April 1983

Walkabout in Melbourne, Australia, April 1983

Perth, Australia, April 1983

Above and right: Maroochydore, Queensland, Australia, April 1983

Ayers Rock, Australia,
April 1983

Sunset over Ayers Rock, Australia, April 1983

TEAMWORK ON TOUR

After the heat and dust of Australia, Charles and Diana found New Zealand damp and dispiriting. The crowds were smaller, and the royal couple were extremely tired. But they were also by now an experienced team, cheerfully rubbing noses in a traditional Maori sign of greeting and traveling in a war canoe. So many warriors jumped into the canoe with them that it almost sank. Diana's confidence had been bolstered by her success in Australia, and I noticed she was much more cheerful. When a Maori "chief" charged at them with a spear in the traditional challenge to strangers, Diana at first backed away, saying, "Goodness, I thought he was going to stab me!" Then she collapsed with laughter.

A garden party in Auckland, New Zealand, April 1983

Above and right: Bay of Islands, New Zealand, April 1983

Touring with a Tot

APRIL 1983

As they were going to be in the South Pacific for six weeks, Charles and Diana decided to take nine-month-old Prince William with them. Despite reports to the contrary, the Queen posed no opposition to Diana's wish to take William along. During the trip, the baby prince learned to crawl and delighted his proud parents, not to mention all of us photographers, by demonstrating his new skill at a press photo call. Charles described their delight in a letter to friends, explaining that when their son crawled for the first time, "We laughed and laughed with sheer, hysterical pleasure." The baby was, he added, "the greatest possible fun." Auckland, New Zealand, April 1983

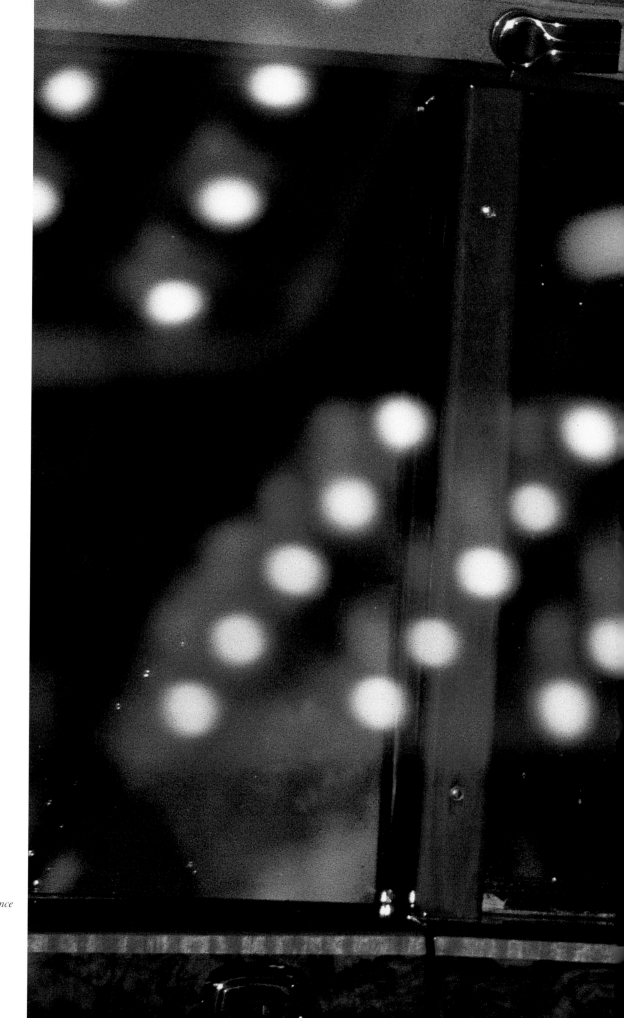

*In the royal limousine after a ballet performance
in Auckland, New Zealand, April 1983*

*On their second wedding anniversary, the Princess watches her
husband playing polo at Cowdray Park in West Sussex. July 1983*

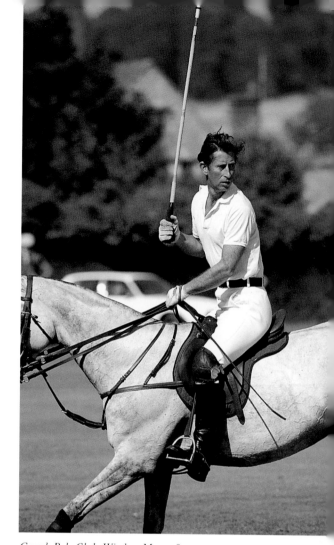

Guards Polo Club, Windsor, May 1983

A DEVOTED WIFE

Diana's devotion to her husband was evident when she spent endless summer Sundays watching him play polo, a game she found boring. Her only enjoyment was chatting with the other players' wives. Her loyalty was impressive, but it ruined our weekends because we were "permitted" to cover the matches.

The Princess waits patiently in the pony lines at Cowdray Park. July 1983

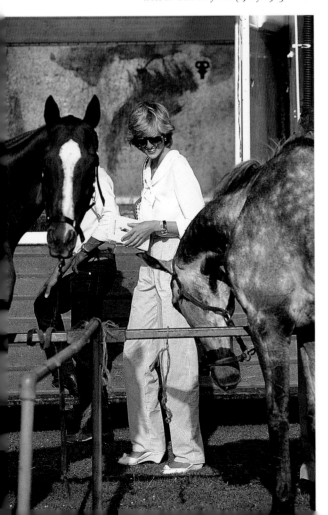

The Prince and Princess followed by Sarah Ferguson at the Guards Polo Club, Windsor, May 1983

WILLIAM MEETS THE PRESS

MAY 1984

At a photo call to mark his second birthday, I was amazed that William happily posed for us photographers, a rather daunting crowd of strangers for a tot to face. Eager for a close-up of our equipment, he peered through viewfinders and inspected television microphone booms, as his proud parents watched. I noticed that the toddler prince constantly scratched his head with his left hand, so I wondered if he would turn out to be a southpaw, which later proved to be correct. As time went on, William's relationship with cameramen deteriorated, and he came to loathe photo calls with us. Kensington Palace, London, May 1984

West End, London, August 1984

Kings College Hospital, London, August 1984

Diana already knows she is expecting her second child, although it has not yet been publicly announced. Norway, February 1984

THE SECOND TIME AROUND

FEBRUARY – AUGUST 1984

Aberdeen airport, Scotland, August 1984

Diana had looked like a galleon in full sail during her first pregnancy but was determined to stay slimmer and more elegant when expecting her second baby. She worked almost up to Prince Harry's birth, did not put on as much weight, and chose a wardrobe of cleverly cut outfits to minimize her ballooning shape. Later she revealed that she and Charles became much closer in the months before their second son's birth. It was a happy time that was to be very short-lived.

Royal Academy, London, May 1984

JUST WILD ABOUT HARRY

Birth announcement outside Buckingham Palace, London, September 1984

The birth of Prince Harry on September 15, 1984, secured the line of succession to the throne. Diana had presented her husband with both an heir and a spare. The royal couple looked delighted as they left the Lindo Wing of St. Mary's Hospital less than 24 hours after their second son's arrival. Their first baby's birth had been announced in a gold-framed statement posted outside Buckingham Palace, as befitting the arrival of a future king; Harry's debut rated only a wood-framed announcement.

William and his father, St. Mary's Hospital, London, September 1984

Crowds outside St. Mary's Hospital, London, September 1984

Leaving St. Mary's Hospital with Prince Harry, London, September 1984

FOR LOYALTY

1985–1990

Arriving at Melbourne airport, after a 24-hour flight from London — so different from the arrival on their first tour of Australia, when they brought baby Prince William, Australia, October 1985

THE SHOW MUST GO ON

Marriage and motherhood began to change Diana. Still desperately insecure and depressed, she decided that her salvation lay in a more serious image. She began to regret bitterly self-deprecating comments she had made, such as a remark to a 16-year-old boy at an orphanage who told her he was worried about passing his exams. Diana confessed that she had never earned a single pass: "Brain the size of a pea, I've got."

This was just a jokey way of putting a nervous youngster at ease, but it lingered in the public's mind. Diana was perceived by many as just a delicious dimwit, an empty-headed Sloane Ranger who cared about nothing but babies and boutiques.

The Forum, Rome, Italy, April 1985

Charles grumbled about the "unutterable rubbish written about my wife." Who could blame him? Newspapers and magazines were filled with endless reports of Diana's wardrobe and weight-watching. Pictures of the Princess in a stunning new outfit made big bucks, so we were always focusing on her fashions. As a female photographer, I took an even greater interest in Diana's designer clothes.

Diana's big dilemma was summed up by the London *Sunday Times*: "How is she ever – short of abandoning her blonde highlights, gaining a couple of stone and slobbering around in unprincesslike clothes – to be taken as anything more than an exquisitely coifed airhead?"

Unfortunately, such stories only increased the Princess's lack of self-worth and her rampant bulimia. But, there was another, less obvious reason she wanted to kill off her frivolous image. The exposure to people from all walks of life – the talented and the terminally ill, the disabled and the dispossessed – had made Diana a more thoughtful woman. She loathed her reputation as a dumb belle but mostly managed to keep her feelings hidden. Her simmering annoyance boiled over one day on a 1985 tour of Italy as she trailed around the architectural glories of Florence after her husband's toffee-nosed dignitaries made it clear they thought she was no culture vulture.

One morning, as they walked through a low arch, Charles warned, "Mind your head!" Diana replied, "Why? There's nothing in it." Her bitter crack was a symptom of her growing resentment. She was bored by dinners with elderly royal officials that dragged on for hours. She was irritated by stuffy royal rules and angry about the lack of personal freedom, although too loyal to show it. The same year, in a television interview she talked fondly about Charles: "I feel my role is supporting my husband whenever I can and always being behind him, encouraging him. And also, most important, being a mother and a wife. And that's what I try to achieve." Then her feelings of inadequacy leaked out as she added, "Whether I do is another thing, but I do try."

But had she still found royal life difficult? "Yes, purely because there was so much attention on me when I first arrived on the scene and I wanted to get my act together, so to speak, and I had so many people watching me, the pressure was enormous. But as the years go on, it gets better," she fibbed.

Although publicly faithful to Charles and his ideals, privately she was disillusioned with her marriage. As if in a reversal of the Grimm fairy tale, Diana felt she had kissed a prince only to find he had turned into a frog. Still in love with her husband, she fretted when Charles spent endless hours in his Highgrove garden and enjoyed evenings with his nose in a book. In an attempt to share his pastimes, she made a photographic record of his work in their garden and did needlework while he read philosophical tomes.

This domestic scene was not how she had imagined life would be like with the world's most glamorous man. Occasionally, she could not contain her frustration any longer and a revealing comment would pop out. In 1985 Diana admitted that as a naive teenager, she simply did not realize what lay in store. As she told a fellow guest at a charity lunch, "One day I was riding to work on a number nine bus, then suddenly all this happened." And with a sweep of one hand she indicated her elevated position at the top table under the relentless scrutiny of the crowded room. She also began to flirt with other men, perhaps to make her husband jealous and therefore more attentive. It was around this time that her suspicion that Camilla Parker Bowles was once again involved with Charles hardened into certainty. It was a devastating blow to her self-esteem but slowly, quietly Diana decided to fight back.

Like many other women in their mid-20s, Diana wanted to make her life more fulfilling. Doting on her children and spending hours in the royal nursery was wonderful, but she had begun to ask herself: Is that all there is?

Finding some meaningful way to assert herself became more urgent when her husband became more distant. Perhaps

The Princess curtseys to Queen Sofia of Spain, Madrid, Spain, April 1987

The Vatican, Rome, Italy, April 1985

Gatwick, Sussex, April 1987

London, May 1989

Italian photographers go wild trying to get pictures of the Princess. "Bella Diana," they call to her. Florence, Italy, April 1985

Vancouver, Canada, May 1986

he would take her seriously if the rest of the world did, so she began searching for more rewarding work. She learned sign language so that she could be a better patron of the British Deaf Association. "I think it's important to show that you're interested and you're not just breezing in and out," she explained. She wanted to learn how people who are deaf cope with a world that doesn't always want to know about them, she went on.

In a bid to kill off "Diana the darling of the dress designers," she began wearing one old outfit after another. After one photographer bluntly asked why she was wearing a "boring old dress," Diana got snippy. "I suppose you'd like it better if I came naked," she replied.

Shaking off her old, unflattering image was not easy. It was not until she found a cause to which she could really commit herself that she found a solution. It was the biggest medical story of the 1980s – AIDS.

When Diana first suggested she should do something to help sufferers of the world's most feared disease, palace advisers discouraged her. She ignored their advice and, in a 1987 visit to the Middlesex Hospital in London, shook hands with an AIDS patient. It was undoubtedly the most significant act by a member of the royal family in a hundred years. Her compassion for sufferers of an illness that many people regarded as self-inflicted transformed attitudes overnight. At last, Diana had achieved something worthwhile. By helping those who were reviled and rejected as social outcasts, she had made a real contribution.

Her success, however, helped only to widen the ever-growing rift between herself and her husband. Diana had only to turn up at a hospital or film premiere to make the front pages day after day, while Charles's own good works went largely unrecognized. She totally overshadowed her more important spouse, and he did not like it.

Soon she swapped her low-heeled pumps for spiky high heels that made her six feet tall, a sign that she no longer cared if she towered over her five-foot-ten-inch husband. Diana's love and loyalty were wearing thin, but still the public pretense of an ideal partnership went on. ∞

Molfetta, Italy, April 1985

The Princess's luggage, Cameroon, Africa, March 1990

Budapest, Hungary, May 1990

ITALIAN STYLE

APRIL 1985

La Spezia, Italy, April 1985

Annoyed by false reports that she had spent a small fortune on new fashions for a tour of Italy, the Princess wore many old clothes. Newspapers called Diana a "Second-Hand Rosa" and claimed she was "Pasta her Besta," criticizing her copy of an Italian waiter's outfit and an oft-seen pink ballgown she wore to the opera at La Scala. But she happily donned an old-fashioned ankle-length gown and black lace mantilla for an audience with Pope John Paul II in the Vatican. The tour opened in Sardinia and ended in Venice, when William and Harry flew out to join their parents for a short cruise around the Mediterranean aboard the royal yacht, *Britannia*. April 1985

Rome, Italy, April 1985

Venice, Italy, April 1985

Venice, Italy, April 1985

Flying Down South

SEPTEMBER 1985

After her annual holiday at the Queen's Highland estate,
Balmoral, Diana returned to London with one-year-old
Prince Harry. Despite heavy rain and windy weather, the
baby prince went barefoot, in keeping with the royal custom
of leaving royal tots unshod until they have learned to walk.
Aberdeen airport, September 1985

FIRST DAY OF SCHOOL

SEPTEMBER 1985

*Inside Mrs. Mynor's Montessori, London,
September 1985*

At just over three years old, it was a big ordeal for a little prince to
have to face his first day at school and a large gathering of press
when he arrived at Mrs. Mynor's Montessori. William was reluctant
to leave the security of his mother's hand as his new headmistress
ushered him into school. By lunchtime, however, he raced out of the
school looking confident and very happy. Mrs. Mynor's Montessori,
London, September 1985

SIGNS OF DISTRESS

OCTOBER 1985

On a second visit to Australia, Diana was bitterly unhappy, as her relationship with Charles went steadily downhill. But she put on a convincing show of togetherness by gazing into Charles's eyes as they danced at a ball in Melbourne. In turn, he was irked by the adulation accorded his wife, who continued to pull vast, worshiping crowds while he was completely upstaged. Diana was startlingly slim, showing all the classic signs of suffering from an eating disorder, but dazzled observers simply believed she was trying to stay fashionably slender. Melbourne, Australia, October 1985

GOING SOLO

OCTOBER 1985

Diana gradually began to make solo trips abroad and enjoyed a visit alone to the Royal Hampshire Regiment's base in Berlin. As the regiment's colonel-in-chief, she took the wheel of a tank and had fun pretending to run down the photographers in her path. When her regiment was later disbanded, she was very upset. Increasingly, it seemed that Diana blossomed when out on her own. Meanwhile, Charles was also making more and more solo trips, and they soon began leading separate lives. Berlin, Germany, October 1985

Above, left, and right: Berlin, Germany, October 1985

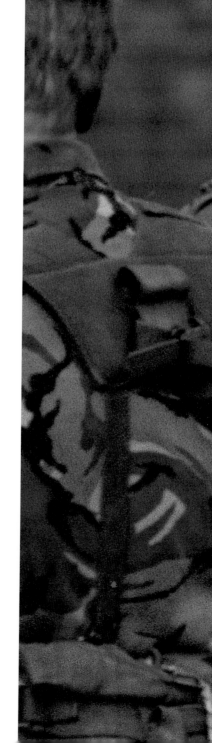

Dinner with Vice President and Mrs. Bush, British Embassy, Washington, D.C., November 1985

WINNING OVER THE STATES

NOVEMBER 1985

Saturday Night Fever broke out in Washington when Diana danced with John Travolta at a White House dinner in November 1985. To her delight, Clint Eastwood was the next to cut in, while Charles did a majestic waltz with Nancy Reagan. The star-studded trip ended in Palm Beach, where they attended a fundraising dinner organized by the billionaire Armand Hammer. Diana looked touchingly young and out of place dining with Hammer's elderly friends, but Charles had a good time dancing with film star Joan Collins.

Polo match, Palm Beach, Florida, November 1985

With President and Mrs. Reagan, White House, Washington, D.C., November 1985

Right: Dinner at the British Embassy, Washington, D.C., November 1985

WHO'S THAT GIRL?

FEBRUARY 1986

Attention is diverted away from the Prince and Princess when Sarah Ferguson
arrives to watch the photo call. Diana glances over at her as she approaches. The
photographers get excited and rush off to take pictures of Sarah instead. Klosters,
Switzerland, February 1986

A MODEL PRINCESS

APRIL 1986

Diana seemed subdued and even more slender when she flew to Austria aboard the Concorde on a goodwill visit in April 1986. Diana was clearly annoyed with Austrian actress Dagmar Killer, the wife of the local mayor, when she flirted openly with a bemused Prince Charles. This was the period of "Dynasty Di," and at a fashion show at the Hofburg Palace, Diana told one top model, "I would love to have been on the catwalk with you today." She commented on the overwhelming smell of hairspray and acidly remarked that her husband had banned her from using it out of his concern for the ozone layer.

Left and right: Vienna, Austria, April 1986

ORDEAL IN THE ORIENT

MAY 1986

The royal wedding had been watched by even more people in Japan than it had in Britain, and as Charles and Diana's six-day tour approached, the country was in a fever of excitement. Diplomatically, her dress was printed with the rising sun symbol as a tribute to her hosts as she flew in. They arrived after a 13-hour flight from Canada, where the Princess, in the grip of bulimia, had fainted while visiting Expo 86. Greeted by Prince Hiro, who was second-in-line to the Chrysanthemum throne, Diana said she felt "okay." After a day off to rest, she launched into an arduous schedule in which she carried out 29 engagements, often being on duty up to 12 hours a day. At Nija Castle in Kyoto, she watched a traditional tea ceremony, then poured a cup for her husband. Afterward she was presented with a $40,000 silk kimono, and after much persuasion, she tried it on for delighted photographers. It was far too long even for a statuesque princess, and Diana made the Japanese giggle as she tottered around trying not to trip while modeling her new gown. Tokyo, Japan, May 1986

The Princess has the giggles as a translator continues interpreting her chat to Emperor Hirohito at a state banquet. Imperial Palace, Tokyo, Japan, May 1986

DAZZLING THE DESERT KINGDOMS

NOVEMBER 1986

On a tour of the Arabian Gulf, Diana was granted a freedom denied to other women in the desert kingdoms. She was invited to King Fahd's palace, a rare honor for a member of her sex, although she was not allowed to dine with the men. The Sultan of Oman presented Diana with a queen's ransom in jewels and gave Charles an Aston Martin sports car. But the royal couple outraged the locals when they perfunctorily kissed after a polo match, a sight that was banned from local TV screens lest it inflame Arab passions.

   Diana's obstetrician, George Pinker, turned up at a banquet, creating reports by the traveling British press that a third baby could be on the way. Diana wrecked their hopes when, looking surprised, she asked, "George! What are you doing here?" He had flown in for a friend's wedding.

Saudi Arabia, November 1986

Riyadh airport, Saudi Arabia, November 1986

Right: A traditional desert picnic, Riyadh, Saudi Arabia, November 1986

Muscat, Oman, November 1986

MIDDLE EASTERN MANNERS

NOVEMBER 1986

At the Omani Women's Association, Muscat, Oman, November 1986

The contrast between Western and Middle Eastern dress codes struck me forcibly when Diana met female students at Muscat University. Diana tried to conform by wearing concealing clothes but still exposed her neck and left her head uncovered. At night she did appear in long-sleeved demure dresses specially made for the Gulf States. November 1986

Saudi Arabia, November 1986

Meeting female students at Muscat University, Muscat, Oman, November 1986

Fashion Parade

Diana's Sergeant Pepper uniform, by designer Catherine Walker, looked smarter than those of any of the soldiers on parade at Sandhurst. But she disliked the fact that what she wore attracted more attention than what she did and wore it only one more time. Slowly, Diana had come to resent her image as a frivolous follower of fashion and began aiming for a more serious image. Sandhurst Military Academy, April 1987

THE REIGN IN SPAIN

APRIL 1987

The relaxed mood of the Spanish King Juan Carlos and his wife, Queen Sofia, astonished Charles and Diana. On a spring 1987 visit, they were whisked around in the King's minivan rather than in royal limousines. On a visit to one of Europe's oldest universities, in Salamanca, Diana was overcome by the heat and needed a ten-minute rest and a drink of water before she could go on. But she brightened when chivalrous students dressed in medieval troubadour costumes threw down their cloaks for her. Significantly, at the end of the tour Diana flew home alone while Charles enjoyed a break in Italy. April 1987

Salamanca University, Salamanca, Spain, April 1987

In the quiet of the polo lines and the horse box park, Prince Harry has his first introduction to polo. He seems more interested in having piggyback rides and playing around in the horse box with his brother than watching the game his father loves to play so much. Princes William and Harry are both accomplished horsemen now but have yet to start to play polo. Guards Polo Club, Windsor, May 1987

Cartier Polo, Guards Polo Club, Windsor, July 1987

WEDDED BLISS

For a few years in the 1980s Charles and Diana were the world's most glamorous, amorous couple. The Prince seized every opportunity to show the world that he loved his wife. He always kissed her when she presented him with trophies after games of polo, or when they parted for even a short time. Diana's smile and the gleam in her eyes as he leaned close revealed not just her own enjoyment, but her delight in his public display of affection. But soon the tension between them became evident, and by the end of the 80s their kisses had become just a formality.

At a charity match at the Royal Berkshire Polo Club in 1991, Prince Charles played on opposing teams to Major James Hewitt. The Princess was not there to watch the match so the Duchess of York presented the prize to Charles's winning team. In 1995 the Princess revealed her love affair with the dashing Major during her famous Panorama television interview. Royal Berkshire Polo Club, July 1991

Cartier Polo, Guards Polo Club, Windsor, July 1987

Sisters-in-Law

June 1987

Longing for a pal at the palace, Diana played Cupid to arrange the match between her friend Fergie and her brother-in-law Prince Andrew in 1985. The two women soon became each other's closest confidantes and together railed against the limitations of court life. The Duchess of York later recalled that her one true friend at Buckingham Palace was Diana, "with whom I shared the outsider's bond. Together we chafed at the conventions that confined us. I will never forget the night we liberated the Queen Mother's Daimler at Balmoral and did gravel spins all the way around the castle. Together we laughed and cried." Epsom, Derby, June 1987

A CLOSE FRIEND

Mohamed Al Fayed, the Egyptian tycoon who owns Britain's most famous store, Harrods, was a close friend of Diana's father, Earl Spencer, and had known the Princess since she was eight years old. In July 1987 he sponsored a polo game at the Guards Polo Club in Windsor Great Park and stood by beaming as Diana presented her husband with the winner's trophy and a kiss. Exactly ten years later, he watched romance blossom between his eldest son, Dodi, and Diana on a vacation at the Fayed family's villa in St. Tropez.
Harrods Polo Match, Guards Polo Club, Windsor, July 1987

SUN, SAND, AND UNDER SIEGE

On a holiday in Majorca as guests of Spain's King Juan Carlos, Diana and Charles agreed to a family photo call in exchange for their being left in peace by the paparazzi thereafter. The ploy did not work, and each time they ventured outside Marivent Palace, the Spanish royal family's seaside villa, they were blitzed by continental photographers. Eventually, to avoid the press, they opted each year to spend their summer vacation cruising through the Greek islands aboard a luxury yacht. August 1987

A Head of Style

At first, few people recognized Princess Diana when she arrived in Caen. She had hidden her famous blond bob beneath a stunning red hat and black snood. She later explained that her hairstylist was away on vacation, and to stay ahead of style she covered up her lank locks. France, September 1987

DIANA'S DREAMS

NOVEMBER 1987

"What would you like to do if you weren't the Princess of Wales?" I asked the Princess when we were having a cozy chat. "I'd really love to become a marriage guidance counselor," she said. "I am a great listener, and I feel I could help a lot of people to sort out their problems."

Above and left: Attending a ballet performance, Berlin, Germany, November 1987

117

A Marriage
that Must Work

NOVEMBER 1987

It was bitterly cold when the Prince and Princess arrived in Berlin
for a six-day visit in November. The royal couple had spent a great
deal of the fall at separate ends of Great Britain, leading to further
reports that their marriage was under strain. But their teamwork
impressed everyone, including sharp-eyed observers like my press
colleagues. We all believed this marriage had to work and that
divorce was out of the question, so they fooled us completely. Diana
later observed, "We had unique pressures put upon us, and we both
tried our hardest to cover them up, but obviously it wasn't to be."
Germany, November 1987

Above and right: Munich, Germany, November 1987

Mr. & Mrs. Perfect Abroad

JANUARY 1988

At Buckingham Palace banquets or on tours abroad, Charles and Diana made a dazzling couple. He looked dashing in white tie and tails, and she shimmered beside him in satin and lace with a tiara gleaming in her hair. No other couple on earth could equal their unique blend of status and sex appeal, and the British government could not possibly have had better ambassadors.

From Madrid to Melbourne, the future King and his alluring wife were a winning team. When Diana turned on her high-voltage charm, every woman was outclassed and every man mesmerized. Australia, January 1988

THAI DI

FEBRUARY 1988

Royal palace, Bangkok, Thailand, February 1988

On a trip to Thailand, Diana remained coolly elegant in the steamy heat. Once again she was the center of attention while her husband was relegated to the role of her escort. "Thai Di!" screamed the delighted locals at every event they attended. The Princess seemed enchanted by her exotic surroundings and carefully hid her growing unhappiness with her husband. At the end of their visit, Charles flew off to Tanzania on safari with friends, and Diana went home alone.

Arriving at the Bangkok airport,
Thailand, February 1988

King's banquet, Bangkok,
Thailand, February 1988

These pages: The Princess visits the practice maneuvers of the Royal Hampshire Regiment of which she is colonel-in-chief, Salisbury Plain, July 1988

PRINCE CHARLES'S 40TH BIRTHDAY PORTRAITS

AUGUST 1988

With his dog Tigger, Highgrove, August 1988

Diana was late arriving at Highgrove, the country home of the Prince and Princess of Wales, where I was waiting to take the official portraits for Prince Charles's 40th birthday, which is actually on November 14th.

When she finally drove up in her car, she was wearing a black satin Michael Jackson "Thriller" jacket. She hurried upstairs to change into something more appropriate for the official photo call. Ten minutes later she came down wearing a demure pink dress and gently chided her husband for wearing a rather worn sweater (right). "You can't be photographed in that old thing!" The Prince laughed, "I don't care. I like it."

Later, as I began to focus my camera, I saw Diana put her arm through his and cuddle up to her husband. There was no sign of the marital problems reported in the press. To me, they seemed like an ordinary, happy couple – affectionate, relaxed, and teasing.

The children, who had been out riding their ponies, were called back from the stables to change for the photo session. I had met the boys a few days earlier at Diana's suggestion so they wouldn't feel shy or nervous while I was shooting. For the photo call, I decided to pack a bag of tricks from a practical-joke shop including an arrow that appears to go straight through the skull of the wearer. Prince Charles put it on and pranced about behind me to make his sons laugh as I photographed them with Diana.

At Highgrove, August 1988

124

Highgrove Estate, Gloucestershire

When we went inside the house to take more pictures, Diana crawled around the floor helping me plug my lights into power sockets around the sitting room. Meanwhile, William and Harry began "helping" me take my camera equipment out of its case and Diana kept ordering them, "Don't touch Jayne's gear." The little boys took no notice, of course.

When we finally finished the session, Diana asked if I would like to stay for lunch with the family. I politely thanked her but turned down the invitation. "You get so little time to be alone together," I explained. "I don't want to intrude." Little did I know that Diana was desperate for some company her own age.

Left and right: Highgrove, August 1988

FRENCH FLAIR

*River cruise on the Seine, Paris, France,
November 1988*

Paying tribute to the capital of chic, Diana crossed the English Channel in Chanel on her first official visit to Paris, in November 1988. A few weeks earlier she had told me she was feeling nervous about the impending trip. "I don't speak French," she explained, "so I am going to wear Chanel from top-to-toe when I arrive." The Parisians adored her, and the city's mayor at the time, Jacques Chirac, raved that he was enchanted by her blue eyes.

One of the highlights of their visit to France was a moonlit cruise down the River Seine aboard that tourists' delight, a bateau-mouche, floating past some of the most famous landmarks in Paris. But it was hardly a romantic evening, as the Prince and Princess exchanged hardly a word throughout the entire meal. Paris, France, November 1988

Elysée Palace, Paris, France, November 1988

Armistice ceremony, Paris,
France, November 1988

PROPER LITTLE PRINCES

Princes William and Harry, Trooping the Colour, London, June 1989

William and Harry had some early lessons in proper behavior for little princes, shaking hands with well-wishers in Canada, riding in royal carriages, carrying bouquets for their mother, and accompanying her to church on Christmas morning. Charles and Diana were gently trying to introduce their sons to the life of duty that lay ahead of them. After Harry shyly met well-wishers outside St. James Cathedral, Toronto, I heard his father whisper, "That was very well done, Harry."

Princes William and Harry on a walkabout for their first official overseas tour, Toronto, Canada, October 1991

Prince Harry at Sandringham, Norfolk, December 1990

QUEEN OF THE DESERT KINGDOM

MARCH 1989

A year and a half before Saddam Hussein invaded Kuwait, Charles and Diana visited the oil-rich state where Diana was treated like a queen and given a chest full of gold jewelry, a silver tea set, and a gold-embroidered Bedouin gown. When she tried it on, about 60 photographers surged forward to capture Desert Queen Diana. In the crush, stepladders went flying and several people were injured. Somehow I emerged with the only clear shot of the Princess in her golden gown. The six-day tour also included the United Arab Emirates and ended in Dubai, from where Diana once again flew home alone. Charles took off on a private visit to Saudi Arabia, where he went painting in the desert.

Kuwait Towers, March 1989

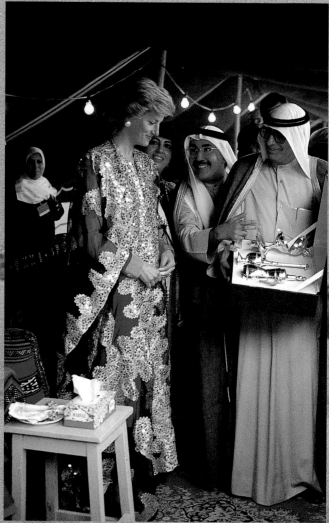

Al-Ain desert, U.A.E., March 1989

With the Crown Prince in Kuwait, March 1989

133

Before the Trooping the Colour ceremony, Kensington Palace, London, June 1989. The Prince and Princess used this image on their Christmas card that year.

TROOPING THE COLOUR

1982 – 1992

The Horse Guards Parade, Trooping the Colour, London, June 1990

The Queen's birthday is officially marked each June by a colorful military parade known as Trooping the Colour. It takes place on Horse Guards Parade off Whitehall in front of crowds and onlookers. The ceremony goes back to the early 18th century, when guards and sentries were mounted daily by the Horse Guards. Each day the colors, or flags, of the battalion, which served as rallying points in battle, were "trooped" slowly down the ranks so that they could be seen and recognized by soldiers in battle. In 1748 it was decided that this parade would take place on the sovereign's birthday, and from the time of George IV, it became an annual event. Until 1986 the Queen took the salute on horseback as the color was trooped past. Since then she has been driven in a phaeton carriage around the parade ground to the saluting base. Members of the royal family, including Diana, until her separation from Charles, also drove in carriages from Buckingham Palace to Horse Guards for the ceremony, which they watched from windows above the parade ground.

1982

1983

1986

1987

1990

1991

Prince Harry at the Horse Guards Parade, Trooping the Colour, London, June 1988

Right: Diana appears with the royal family on the balcony at Buckingham Palace to watch the ceremonies. Trooping the Colour, June 1982-1992

1984

1985

1988

1989

1992

Royal Ascot race meeting, June 1988

Diana seems to float above the sea of people in the paddock enclosure. Royal Ascot race meeting, June 1989

Eastern Delights

New Territories, Hong Kong, November 1989

On her arrival in Hong Kong, Diana let the East go to her head, wearing a hat with a temple-topped crown. Her delighted Chinese hosts invited her to paint in the eye of a dragon for good luck, and the daughters of Gurkha tribesmen decked her with colorful garlands. Cheering, clapping crowds greeted her everywhere, uncharacteristic behavior for the normally reserved Chinese, who dubbed Diana "Di On Na Wong Fei," shortened to "Di Wong Fei" *(Diana, royal concubine)*. Incredibly, once again Diana flew home without her husband, who set off on a cruise aboard the royal yacht, *Britannia*, through the South China Sea.

H.M.S. Tamar, *Hong Kong, November 1989*

Despite the steamy heat of Indonesia, Diana enjoyed a trip to Yogyakarta, visiting a sultan and his queen in the middle of the jungle and being moved by the plight of sufferers at a leprosy clinic. Undismayed by the sight of disfigured patients, she sat on their beds and held their hands. The hospital's doctor, Maartin Teterissa, said later, "The Princess has done an enormous service to the world's fifteen million leprosy sufferers by demonstrating that the disease is fully curable by drugs, and that it is contagious only through many years of constant and prolonged contact."

Above and left: Tamrin Mini, Jakarta, Indonesia, February 1989

WORKING FOR BRITAIN

MARCH 1990

Lagos Hospital, Nigeria, March 1990

Throbbing African drums, tribal dancers, and stifling heat greeted a wilting Diana on a five-day visit to Nigeria in March 1990. Nevertheless, she looked cool in a dress of green and white, the Nigerian national colors. Although she enjoyed meeting the governor's wife, Madame Ankanobi, at a cultural show at the Old Lodge in Enugu, the Princess soon realized why the country was once known as "the White Man's grave." In Maiduguri the royal couple, loaded with anti-typhoid and yellow fever shots, endured hours under a baking sun in 110°F heat. They had to watch a *durbar*, which is an official assembly of two thousand horsemen, who stirred up a cloud of dust thundering up and down a parade ground in front of the tired, thirsty royal visitors.

Lagos, Nigeria, March 1990

With traditional dancers, Enugu, Nigeria, March 1990

Lagos, Nigeria, March 1990

145

Port Harcourt, Nigeria, March 1990

AFRICAN MISSION

MARCH 1990

Bamenda, Nigeria, March 1990

Looking like a prim missionary's wife, Diana visited a school for the deaf in Cameroon and demurely applauded a welcoming speech at a civic reception. As French is the country's main language, an eight-year-old student greeted her with the words, "Bienvenue, Altesse, à notre école" *(Welcome, Highness, to our school)*. Diana, who did not speak French, said, laughing, "Even I can understand that!" Following a visit to neighboring Nigeria, Diana was exhausted from the sweltering 120°F heat. Her mood did not improve when the air conditioning aboard the royal yacht, *Britannia*, on which she was staying, broke down after hordes of jellyfish were sucked into its underwater cooling vents.

Yaoundé Deaf School, Cameroon, March 1990

147

BANQUET BLUES

Diana asked me to take some official portraits that she and Charles would give as gifts to foreign dignitaries and heads of state. She suggested that I come to Kensington Palace one evening when they were all dressed up for a state banquet.

I was told to set up my cameras in the dining room. A table covered with a plastic, patterned Laura Ashley cloth had been shoved to one side of the room to create enough space for the photo session. Diana soon appeared wearing a magnificently embroidered lilac gown and a tiara. When I admired her dress, she groaned. "It's so tight I can barely breathe," she explained. "I don't know how I'll be able to survive the banquet. If I eat anything, the dress will get even tighter. I am dreading the whole evening."

Prince Charles eventually arrived wearing a dress uniform and a chest full of medals. As I began to light the picture I jokingly asked him, "What did you have to do to get all those medals?" Before he could say a word, Diana muttered some comment under her breath. Prince Charles betrayed not a flicker of annoyance, but less than five minutes later the photo call was over. London, March 1990

*With sons at Nottingham Hospital, London,
September 1990*

AN UNLUCKY BREAK

When Prince Charles shattered his arm in a polo accident, Diana took William and Harry to visit their father in the hospital. Later she took him home after more treatment in Nottingham. When she took the children back to school in London, the press reported that Camilla Parker Bowles was a frequent visitor to the ailing Prince.

Cirencester Hospital, London, July 1990

A HEALING TOUCH

Hull, Humberside, June 1992

In a manner unprecedented in the royal family, Diana appreciated the power of touch. While the Queen, her sister, and her daughter swanned through royal duties wearing gloves when shaking hands, Diana almost never wore them. She liked to get close to the people, embracing children and old people alike. Her talent for sharing ordinary people's pleasures set her apart from her royal relatives and reserved husband, and it did much to increase her popularity. "Everybody needs hugs," she once said. Diana's efforts meant so much to people with AIDS and who are HIV-positive, and she helped break down fear and prejudice in Washington by holding an AIDS baby in her arms.

Peto Institute, Budapest, Hungary, May 1990

Foundation for Conductive Education, Birmingham, October 1995

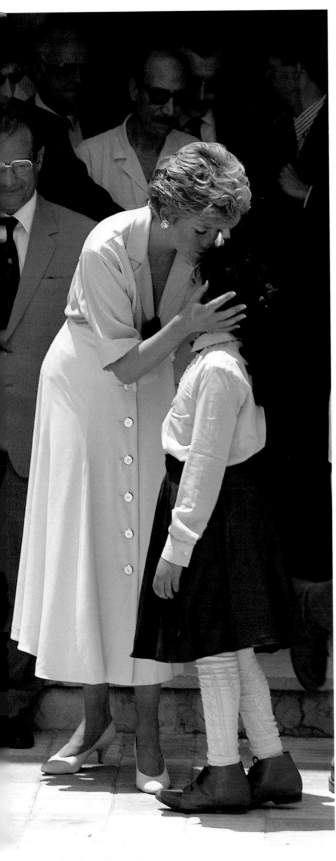

Cairo Institute, Egypt, May 1992

Carrying a girl who is HIV-positive, Washington, D.C., October 1990

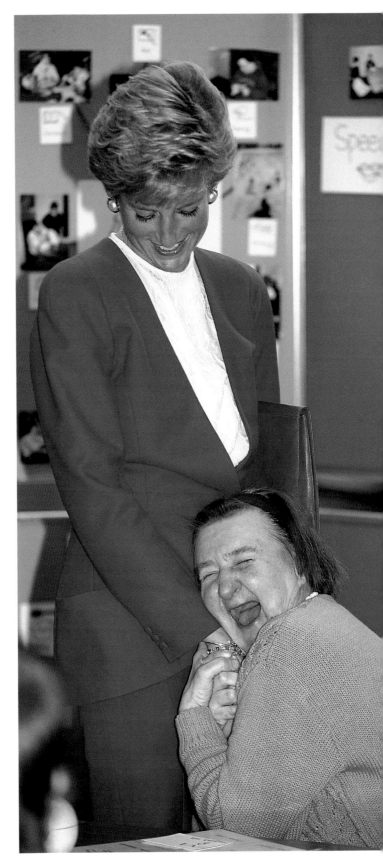

Six Acres Day Center, Taunton, Devon, April 1991

BACK IN THE U.S.A.

Diana dazzled Washington at a gala dinner, where she chatted with First Lady Barbara Bush at the White House and joined her at Grandma's House, a center for people with AIDS and who are HIV positive. Diana's great-grandmother Frances Work, or Fanny, as she was known to her family, was an American, and perhaps that is why the Princess always felt such a great affinity for the land across the Atlantic. Fanny's father began his career as a clerk in Ohio and ended up making millions as a financial whiz in Manhattan. A great patriot, he promised to disinherit any of his offspring who married Europeans. But Fanny, like Diana a strong-willed woman, crossed the Atlantic and married British aristocrat James Boothby Burke Roche, who became the third Baron Fermoy. When the marriage broke up, she returned to New York with twin sons and a daughter, and her indulgent father forgave her.

Above and left: Washington, D.C., October 1990

With Barbara Bush at the White House, Washington, D.C., October 1990

A Welcome Guest

Banquet for the Emperor's enthronement, Tokyo, Japan, November 1990

At the enthronement of Emperor Akihito of Japan, Diana and Charles were downgraded to second-rank royals, as kings, queens, and other heads of state got front-row seats. Diana was relegated to 71st place in the pecking order among 2,500 guests. But Japanese admirers, waiting to catch a glimpse of her, made it clear she was still their favorite.

Workers at a car factory in Tokyo, where she inspected Ayrton Senna's winning Grand Prix racer, gave the Princess a Formula One greeting. Diana had recently been stopped by British police for speeding on a motorway, and one of my colleagues, more cheeky than the rest of us, indicated the car and said, "They'd never catch you on the motorway in that, ma'am." Diana grinned and quipped back, "I'll tell the jokes, thank you." A few days later she saw the same man wearing a tweed cap in a heavy downpour. "Are you wearing that hat for a bet?" she teased. "I'll tell the jokes, thank you, ma'am," he replied.

Arriving at the Emperor's enthronement, Tokyo, Japan, November 1990

Honda factory, Tokyo, Japan, November 1990

In the Red and Pink

Life was always rosy when Princess Diana turned up for an official occasion wearing pink. It was a signal that she was in a warm, happy mood. Diana often wore a bright, blush pink in early spring or late autumn when she wanted to glow on a gray day. When she felt unusually confident, she chose red – a clear, traffic-light shade of sizzling scarlet because she knew it made her stand out in a crowd.

FOR LIBERTY

1991–1997

FREEDOM AT ANY PRICE

S he gave up a crown and a golden page in the history books. To Diana, freedom was worth more than all the status and style of a future queen. As the last decade of the 20th century opened, she made up her mind to escape from the soul-destroying world behind palace walls. Charles and Diana had been estranged for years, so why didn't she walk out earlier? For some time, the fear that she might lose her children forced her to remain in a life she loathed.

The way out was perhaps the most brilliant public relations exercise of the era. Diana enlisted the sympathy and support of the entire world when she leaked the story of her husband's infidelity and her own suicidal despair. "My life is torture," she told friends, who dutifully passed this information on to the press. Buckingham Palace countered such gossip by insisting that all was well between the couple. It took Andrew Morton's bombshell of a book to end the charade of a happy marriage.

After the book was published in June 1992, Diana became a heroine, suffering in saintly silence until worried friends revealed her secret pain, or so everyone supposed. Her royal relatives were convinced that this was far from the truth, even when the Princess briefly denied any involvement in Morton's

Taj Mahal, Agra, India, February 1992

Charles Bridge, Prague, Czechoslovakia, May 1991

Seoul, Korea, November 1992

book. Within days it became apparent that she had authorized the attack on her husband and his mistress when she very publicly visited one of the sources for the book.

In December 1992 the Prime Minister announced the official separation of the Prince and Princess of Wales to a stunned House of Commons. But almost four years would pass before Diana gained her liberty in a London divorce court.

By that time the high price of her freedom made her regret breaking up the marriage. A bitter War of the Waleses had taken its toll. In November 1995 Diana scored a short-lived triumph with a BBC-TV Panorama interview during which she fired a fusillade at Charles, hinting that he should not be king. During the broadcast she delivered one of the most memorable utterances of her life: "There were three of us in the marriage so it was a bit crowded." Suddenly, I realized that Camilla had always been there in the background, like a specter casting a dark shadow over Diana's happiness. Looking back I wonder why we didn't see what was going on much earlier. It took Diana to expose the situation first in Andrew Morton's book and then in her interview. Later, when critics claimed that by attacking the Prince she had damaged her children, she said the interview was a mistake.

She was mad, bad, and dangerous to know, according to courtiers, and gossips spread sizzling stories about the other men in her life. Her reported scandalous friendships with art dealer Oliver Hoare and England's rugby captain Will Carling prompted accusations that she was a heartless schemer manipulating men for her own amusement.

In reality, Diana was in despair. She had realized that instead of escaping from the House of Windsor after her divorce, she was more imprisoned than ever. She had lost the title Her Royal Highness and many of its trappings. She could not leave the country without royal permission, her husband no longer paid the bills for her high-maintenance lifestyle, and her divorce settlement of $35 million seemed totally inadequate to keep her for the rest of her life.

The paparazzi made her life a misery, and I, too, felt disheartened. The Princess made only rare public appearances and, when she did carry out charity work, was, understandably, not always cooperative with the swarms of photographers. It seemed pointless to carry on doing authorized photographs when the media demanded the unofficial, intrusive shots.

Diana faced an uncertain future, and it took a long period of adjustment for her to emerge from a depression brought on by

*On their last tour together, in Korea, pressmen
dubbed the miserable royal couple "the Glums."
It was clear that they could not bear to be with
each other, and it was later revealed that Diana
had agreed to the trip only after the Queen had
insisted that she accompany her husband. Diana's
lady-in-waiting, Anne Beckwith-Smith, later
admitted that she was amazed by the hostility
between the couple. Photographers pleaded for
a shot of Diana and Charles together, so they
promptly walked down separate staircases in a
bid to stay far apart. It was to be their last trip
abroad together. Just weeks later, their sham
marriage came to an end. Pulguksa Temple,
Korea, November 1992*

the end of her royal life. Historically, her position was unprecedented in modern times. Not since the Prussian Princess Caroline was dumped by her husband, the Prince Regent, in 1796 and banned from his coronation in 1821 had a royal lady been so isolated at court.

No longer royal, yet far from being a commoner, she was trapped between two worlds. Diana had lost the backing of the establishment and incurred the deep and abiding hatred of Prince Charles's supporters, who saw her as an enormous threat to his throne. She had also lost the family life she had always envisaged with her husband and sons.

But, despite being downgraded by the Windsors, she remained a winner in the eyes of the world. Many women admired her feisty stance against the British royal family and the establishment. Her work as a charity champion continued to inspire respect and admiration.

To many, Diana represented a kinder, braver side of ourselves. She cared for the lost, the lonely, and the unloved, just as we would all like to believe we would too. The girl who flunked all her exams suddenly became Humanitarian of the Year, proving that you don't need a college degree to make a major contribution to society.

Although far from being a feminist, Diana did a great deal for ordinary women. Through her devotion to her boys, she elevated the role of mother and caretaker to unprecedented heights. Although no longer a member of the royal family, she still overshadowed her former husband and all his relatives. To many people, Diana was the royal family.

Her life took an upturn when she became romantically involved with Pakistani heart surgeon Hasnat Khan in 1995. Her devotion to him taught her at last to understand Prince Charles's passion for Camilla Parker Bowles. From then on, she was more or less reconciled with her ex-husband. The lingering affection they had always shared, despite their battles, returned to bring peace at last after the stormy years.

Her feelings for Dr. Khan began to fizzle out just when Mohamed Al Fayed invited her to join him and his son, Dodi, at their family's villa in St. Tropez in July 1997. She had a new love, and her new crusade against landmines had sparked worldwide support. Her life, she declared, was "pure bliss" just before it was cruelly snuffed out.

Diana was no longer simply the world's most adored princess, she was a legend, destined to be remembered as one of the definitive figures of her time. ❧

Feeding station at the Nemazura refugee camp, Zimbabwe, July 1993

Tgongogora refugee camp, Zimbabwe, July 1993

WILLIAM WALES MEETS THE WELSH

MARCH 1991

During the Gulf War in 1991, Prince Charles canceled a skiing holiday, believing it was not appropriate. Looking for something to do instead, he asked his staff what his wife had planned that week. When informed that Diana was taking Prince William on his first trip to Wales, he decided to join them. They were given a tremendously warm welcome in Cardiff when they went on a walkabout. Diana whispered instructions to eight-year-old William, urging him to shake hands with as many people as possible. But he blushed when young Welsh girls screamed his name and gave him a pop star's welcome.

Diana was constantly explaining that William was extremely camera-shy. "He doesn't like being photographed," she told me. "So, how do you persuade a small boy to behave so beautifully in public?" I asked. "I give him a lot of special coaching to prepare him for each event," she said. "And I also promise him a treat if he's a good boy. For instance, if he does what he's told at the Queen's official parade, I promise to take him to a leisure park." Cardiff, Wales, March 1991

DIANA'S TENTH ANNIVERSARY – ALONE

JULY 1991

By 1991 it was no surprise to find that Charles and Diana planned to spend their tenth wedding anniversary hundreds of miles apart. While he puttered about at their country home, Highgrove, in Gloucestershire, she represented the Queen on the other side of England at the Queen's Review by passing out a parade of cadets at the Royal Air Force base Cranwell.

It was an extremely formal occasion and Diana looked suitably dignified. Once the parade was over, she reverted to her normal self, giggling with her fingers in her ears as a deafening, low-flying Vulcan bomber flew over in salute.

Later, while on a short walkabout among airmen's families, many wished her a happy anniversary, but the Princess made no comment at all. Royal Air Force base, Cranwell, Lincolnshire, July 1991

THE PROBLEMS OF PAKISTAN

Arriving at Norpoor Family Center, Islamabad, Pakistan, September 1991

On her first major solo tour to that region, Diana visited Pakistan, traveling from the Punjab to Peshawar in just four days. In Islamabad she was hailed as a wonderful role model for the mothers of Pakistan, which has a population steadily rising above 120 million, because she had only two children. "I believe mothers will follow your example," Mahbun Ahmed, the Minister for Population and Welfare, told a blushing Diana. President Ishaq Khan explained that Pakistan had more than two million drug addicts, and Diana replied, "It is a scourge all of us need to address. It mostly affects unemployed people and those who have empty lives." But she offended her hosts on a visit to a mosque in Lahore (right) by wearing a knee-length skirt the mullahs considered too short. Pakistan, September 1991

The Khyber Rifles Regiment, 282 Minchi Point, Khyber Pass, Pakistan, September 1991

Badshahi Mosque, Lahore, Pakistan, September 1991

PLAYTIME WITH DIANA

OCTOBER 1991

Children were always the center of Diana's world. Once, on a visit to Oxfordshire, she toured Jaguar's new Super Car headquarters and then turned up at the nearby Queensway Primary School in her own gleaming Jag. One of the young pupils asked if he could sit in her car. Diana said yes, then laughed as a long line of excited children begged for the same treat. With all the firmness of a former nursery school teacher, she opened both back doors and waved the youngsters through in an orderly fashion. Each hopped in one side, wriggled across the plush leather seat, then jumped out through the other door. Banbury, Oxfordshire, October 1991

Diana's Favorite Picture

OCTOBER 1991

The photograph Diana cherished most of all the millions taken of her throughout her royal career was my snap of the Princess aboard the royal yacht, *Britannia*. She had flown to Toronto, where the yacht was moored, two days after her sons, William and Harry, had arrived. She was so happy to see them that she rushed up the gangplank, ran along the deck where they were waiting, and, throwing her arms wide, hugged them to her. Diana asked me for a copy of this shot and hung it in her dressing room at Kensington Palace so that she could see it every day. Toronto, Canada, October 1991

MAID OF THE MIST IV

A Chilly Tour of Canada

OCTOBER 1991

Charles and Diana sparked more stories that their relationship was in serious trouble by barely exchanging a word on a visit to Canada. They looked as miserable as the chilly weather at a civic welcome in Canada. But keeping up the charade of a happy marriage, Charles continued to call his wife "darling" in public. On her only day off that week, Diana took William and Harry, who were on a school break, to Ontario's biggest tourist attraction. "Niagara Falls for Diana," raved the local newspapers. Toronto, Canada, October 1991

Left: Toronto Civic Center, Toronto, Canada, October 1991

175

THE ROYAL KISS-OFF

FEBRUARY 1992

Their final public kiss was more like a kiss-off. In 1992, just a few months before Andrew Morton's bestseller exploded the myth of their happy marriage, Diana watched Charles play polo in Jaipur during a tour of India. After the game, when Diana handed him the winner's trophy, he bent toward her to plant a perfunctory kiss on her lips. At the last second, Diana turned her head in an obvious show of distaste. An embarrassed Charles ended up kissing her ear. Jaipur, India, February 1992

Polo match in Jaipur, India, February 1992

177

CLOSE TO THE END

Sign at Mother Teresa's Hospice for the Sick and Dying, Calcutta, India, February 1992

India proved to be a turning point in Charles and Diana's relationship. As usual, most of the British press followed the Princess, ignoring Charles, who carried out a separate program much of the time. While he talked to business leaders, she broke local taboos by warmly greeting India's lowest of the low, the Untouchables, who flung themselves at Diana's feet. Later, she comforted the dying at Mother Teresa's hospice in Calcutta after Charles had left the country. The nuns there welcomed the Princess with several hauntingly lovely songs. Diana had tears in her eyes as she listened, but she was not alone. The entire press corps was moved to tears by the beauty of their voices. Hardened old hacks from Fleet Street emptied their pockets and gave the sisters all the money they had to continue their wonderful work. Without regard for her pink designer dress, which was covered in dirt from the bare walls, she visited every one of the 50 patients, who were close to death.

Mother Teresa's Hospice for the Sick and Dying in Calcutta, India, February 1992

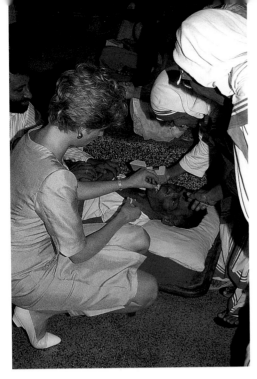

Overleaf: Diana's love for little girls was evident at her meeting with exotically dressed young dancing girls in Hyderabad. The Princess, who seemed to have everything, never realized the dream of having a daughter of her own. Lallapet High School, Hyderabad, India, February 1992

Mother Teresa's Hospice in Calcutta, India, February 1992

With the Untouchables, Hyderabad, India, February 1992

A DAUGHTER'S FAREWELL

MARCH 1992

After the funeral for Diana's father, the eighth Earl Spencer, Charles departed early from the wake that was held at the family home, Althorp, prompting further press rumors that their marriage was ending. Later, his friends revealed that Diana had not wanted him with her at all. But he showed up for the Earl's memorial service at St. Margaret's, Westminster, a few months later. Great Brington, Northamptonshire, March 1992

The pyramids at Giza, Egypt, May 1992

The Sphinx at Giza, Egypt, May 1992

Karnak Temple, Luxor, Egypt, May 1992

OUT OF EGYPT

MAY 1992

On a solo trip to Egypt, Diana chose a beige safari-style dress to visit the Pyramids, reminding me of the scorching days 11 years earlier when I had waited for her to turn up there on her honeymoon. We photographers sighed with frustration, knowing her desert-toned dress would blend in with the sandy background, making her less visible.

Nearby were some camels draped in red, yellow, and green saddle cloths and reins. We promptly hired one to add some color to the rather drab scene and sat back, feeling pleased with our plan, to await Diana's arrival. Just before her car drew up, an overzealous palace official rushed up and demanded that the camel be removed. Later that day I told the Princess what had happened. She laughed, "Yes, of course, I would have posed with the camel – as long as you didn't ask me to sit on it," she said, pulling a face. "Don't forget, I'm wearing a tight skirt." May 1992

Karnak Temple, Luxor, Egypt, May 1992

THE RELUCTANT TOURIST

Above and left: Seoul, Korea, November 1992

By the middle of 1992 Charles and Diana were so hostile to each other that if they found themselves in the same home, they would enter and leave by separate entrances to avoid meeting. They even used separate dining rooms. As a result, Diana at first refused to accompany her husband on a planned tour of Korea scheduled for the fall.

I found it extremely difficult to get a smiling picture of them both. From the minute she arrived, her resentment and loathing were all too obvious. Diana looked so miserable at a banquet in Seoul that my heart went out to her. I looked through my lens and could see she had been crying. Her face was red and blotchy, and her eyes were swimming with unshed tears. Although I watched her intently for almost an hour, I did not see her glance at her husband once. She acted as if he wasn't there.

During this tour, speculation was rife as to whether the Princess had directly helped or been interviewed for Andrew Morton's book. Only a few people were privy to this information, and I was one of them. I had been asked to take some exclusive photographs for a forthcoming book that the Princess had agreed to pose for. I was not aware at that time of the contents of the book but was surprised she had agreed to have new pictures taken for any book. The photo session, however, did not materialize. I think the Princess thought twice about it and realized just how directly it would have shown her involvement. I never told anyone about the proposed photo session as I didn't feel it was for me to comment.

State banquet, Seoul, Korea, November 1992

DEATH OF A MARRIAGE

DECEMBER 9, 1992

Diana put on a brave face and kept smiling at a special school in Tyne and Wear on the day – December 9, 1992 – that British Prime Minister John Major announced that she and Charles had officially separated. Charles had already moved out of their London apartment at Kensington Palace, and Diana had removed her belongings from their country home, Highgrove. She never returned to the house she had once described as "my dream home."

Above and right: Westlawn Special School, Tyne and Wear, December 1992

SPREADING HER WINGS

MARCH 1993

The palace tried to clip Diana's wings after her 1992 separation from Charles. The Queen's aides began spreading the word that her foreign trips on behalf of Britain would be limited from then on. Undeterred, Diana insisted to reporters in early 1993 that she was determined to become a goodwill ambassador for Britain. Without firm backing from the British government, she turned to charities like the Red Cross to organize tours to Third World countries like Zimbabwe and Nepal.

Above and right: Panauti village, Nepal, March 1993

ON TOP OF THE WORLD

Panauti villagers turn out to see the Princess during a Red Cross visit, March 1993

Diana arrived in Nepal under a cloud after fresh revelations of her romance with car dealer James Gilbey and their taped "Squidgygate" telephone conversation were revealed in London. But soon she was literally on top of the world as she visited Red Cross relief projects in the disaster-prone Himalayan state. The high altitude didn't bother her, but it left royal aides panting in her wake. Although her own life had been turned upside down, the Princess forgot her cares as, smiling in a way she had not done for a very long time, she plunged into crowds of Nepali admirers. The tour turned out to be a triumph. Nepal marked a new beginning for Diana, reassuring her that despite the end of her royal marriage, she still had an important role to play as a humanitarian.

Left and right: Site of the Pakistani International Airline plane crash, Nepal, March 1993

A Plea for Time and Space

DECEMBER 1993

On December 3, 1993, Judy Wade telephoned and told me to rush to the Hilton Hotel in London as Diana was about to announce she was quitting public life. In total disbelief, I dashed to Park Lane to find around 60 photographers crammed onto the four-foot-wide pavement at the back entrance to the hotel. Finally, Diana emerged looking sad but relieved. Close to tears, she had appealed for some "time and space" after 13 years in the spotlight. She did cut down on the number of her official engagements, but after a lengthy break, she once again began to do more work for the charities she supported.

ICE QUEEN ON THE
AUSTRIAN SLOPES

MARCH 1994

Above and left: Lech, Austria, March 1994

Diana's winter holidays with her sons were frequently
marred by harassment from continental paparazzi.
Once, in the Austrian Alps in Lech, two Italian photographers chased her down the town's main street trying to
snap pictures. William and Harry became frightened as
their mother confronted the cameramen and told them
to go away. Incidents like this led to William's hatred
and distrust of all photographers.

On another trip to Lech, Diana spotted me looking
at magazines in a shop and stopped to chat. We were
gossiping about everyone we knew for such a long time
that her friend Catherine Soames eventually had to drag
her away.

BACK IN THE FOLD

MAY 1994

Never close to her father-in-law and rarely photographed with him, Diana joined Prince Philip, along with the Queen, at the D-day commemoration service, along with President and Mrs. Clinton. Diana's discomfort was evident as she returned to the royal fold for the day. Portsmouth, May 1994

Canadian Memorial, Green Park, London, May 1994

With Prince Philip at the D-day commemoration service, Portsmouth, May 1994

A BRAVE FRONT

JUNE 30, 1994

The midsummer night when Prince Charles admitted his infidelity with Camilla Parker Bowles on television, Diana knocked him off the world's front pages by wearing a bewitching black gown to an art gallery dinner at the Serpentine in Hyde Park, London. The War of the Waleses was on in earnest with both hurling grenades at each other from their entrenched positions. The next day, the British public, outraged by Charles's candor, voted Diana the victor. June 30, 1994

Above and right: Serpentine Gallery, London, June 1994

Palace of Versailles, Paris, France,
November 1994

Sandringham, Norfolk, Christmas Day 1994

SILENT NIGHT

DECEMBER 1994

Christmas became a lonely time for Diana after her marriage failed. Her children spent the festive season with their father at the Queen's Sandringham estate. In 1992 two weeks after her separation from Charles, she joined her brother's family for the holiday. For the sake of her sons, she first attended church on Christmas morning with the royal family, but in later years stayed alone in London at Kensington Palace. After her divorce became final on August 28, 1996, and unable to bear another sad December 25, she spent her last Christmas Day in the Caribbean with her secretary.

With Liz Tilberis at Lincoln Center,
New York, January 1995

Lincoln Center, New York, January 1995

Chic and Sleek Slick

JANUARY 1995

Diana became a city slicker with a new sleek hairstyle for a gala charity dinner organized in New York by her dear friend Liz Tilberis, the editor-in-chief of *Harper's Bazaar* magazine. Fashion critics claimed the severe hairdo did not flatter her large nose. Back in London, she said she had reluctantly been persuaded to try a new look by her hairstylist. "I'll never do it again," she said. "I was so worried about it that it took about nine people to shove me out the door." Lincoln Center for the Performing Arts, New York, January 1995

London, October 1994

Bergen, Germany, June 1995

Serpentine Gallery, London, June 1995   *Howe Barracks, Canterbury, July 1995*

With John Major at the VJ Day celebrations, London, July 1995

So Near and So Far

JULY 1995

It was to be their last official engagement together as a family when Diana and Charles, accompanied by their sons, attended VJ Day celebrations. To spectators, they looked the very picture of a happy family enjoying an afternoon watching a parade. On this day they put personal differences aside for duty and presented a united family front. London, July 1995

With the Princes at the VJ Day celebrations, London, July 1995

SEPTEMBER 1995

On Prince William's first day at Eton College, Diana and Charles put on a united front with Harry for their son's sake. Diana arrived in the same car as her husband to make the event a family affair. She even smiled happily as they posed together for photographs recording this big day in her elder son's life. Eton College, September 1995

THE QUEEN OF HEARTS

FEBRUARY 1996

Mohamed Al Fayed hosted a dinner at Harrods to raise funds for heart research and especially for the work done at the Papworth Hospital, for which the Princess was a high-profile supporter. She had already been dubbed the Queen of Hearts after comments she had made a few months earlier on her Panorama television interview. Al Fayed seemed enchanted with her, just as his son, Dodi, was to become later.

Charity work for heart transplant surgery and people with AIDS became Diana's main preoccupations after she became romantically involved with Pakistani surgeon Hasnat Khan in 1995. They met when he operated on the husband of her friend Oonagh Toffolo. On a charity trip to Pakistan, she met Dr. Khan's family and wore the *salwar kameez*, the traditional Muslim dress. Diana managed to keep their relationship a secret for almost two years before it was reported in the press. February 1996

Arriving at Harrods dinner with Al Fayed, London, February 1996

LAST MONTHS

In the last year of the Princess's life I only photographed her a few times. I had become disenchanted at the continuous circus of media that seemed to follow her every move. I was also very much against the paparazzi element and disillusioned that no one in authority seemed to want to help. To try to sort out the harassment problem of the Princess and her sons, I had even given the Princess help in preparing for possible legal action to prevent paparazzi intrusion and was willing to be a technical witness for the Princess.

I could always detect her frame of mind when she walked through the door, and often a big clue was the color of her clothes. If she wore dark clothes she was usually not so happy. In October I had taken photographs of her on an exclusive shoot for a magazine at the London Lighthouse. That day she had arrived in a bright red suit, and it was instantly obvious that she was very happy and relaxed. However, my last photographs of her were taken at the headquarters of the English National Ballet in London. She was wearing a dark gray trouser suit and did not seem in a particularly happy mood. She decided to take control of the photo session and began ordering me where to take pictures, insisting on posing on a black sofa. The results were extremely disappointing, especially when she paused for only a few seconds in front of the Christmas tree and said, "I think that's enough now."

Above and left: London Lighthouse AIDS Center,
October 1996

The last photograph I took of Diana, Headquarters of the English National Ballet, London, December 1996

LOWS IN THE HIGHLANDS

AUGUST 1997

Prince William telephoned his mother to discuss his fear of facing 50 photographers for a photo call organized by his father beside the River Dee at Balmoral Castle in August 1997. He little realized that it would be one of their last conversations. While he enjoyed a summer vacation with his father and royal cousins, Diana went on a cruise through the Mediterranean with Dodi Al Fayed aboard his father's yacht, *Jonikal*. She left England on August 21, never to return.

Above and right: Balmoral Castle, Scotland, August 1997

AUGUST 31, 1997

THE LAST JOURNEY

SEPTEMBER 6, 1997

Buckingham Palace's flag flies at half mast, London, September 1997

William and Harry chose to follow their mother's coffin, along with their father and their uncle Earl Spencer, on a mile-long walk to Westminster Abbey. Despite huge crowds lining the route, the only sound that could be heard in the streets was the clip-clop of the horses drawing the gun carriage on which the coffin lay, and the muffled sobbing of the people, including many of the pressmen and presswomen covering the saddest royal event of the century. But my lasting memory of the Princess will always be the laughter in her blue eyes. Despite her troubles, she always managed to smile and frequently joked with those of us in the British press pack. Her lively sense of humor and her kindness lightened the work load for all of us. There will never be anyone else like her – at least not in my lifetime. Diana became a princess but was destined never to be a queen. It hardly matters now, because she will reign in the hearts of all who loved her forever.

Diana's coffin on the gun carriage as it proceeds through the streets of London, September 1997

Public tears at Diana's funeral, London, September 1997

Funeral cortege outside Westminster Abbey, London, September 1997

Preceding page, left to right: Earl Spencer, Princes William and Harry, and the Prince of Wales unite in grief at Westminster Abbey for the funeral. London, September 1997

Left: Diana's coffin leaves Westminster Abbey for the private family burial, London, September 1997

Following pages: Floral and other tributes left for the late Princess. Kensington Palace, September 1997

FLORAL TRIBUTES

I say goodbye one last time to the Princess, Kensington Palace, September 1997

It is a British custom to present royal ladies with a bouquet when they arrive at an official function. Often, such events might include a walkabout, when the Princess would walk along the street greeting well-wishers who regularly showered her with flowers. Diana received so many that she usually quickly had to hand them over to her lady-in-waiting. Sometimes, policewomen would be needed to assist in carrying armfuls of flowers to the Princess's car. Diana usually sent them to nearby hospitals, so that patients could enjoy them, but she also gave some to her staff. She regularly told her chauffeur Simon Solari, "I've kept you out late tonight, so take these home to your wife with my apologies."

Her favorite flowers were white roses and lilies, and wreaths of these blooms from her sons decorated her coffin. In a fitting memorial to the Princess, whose Kensington Palace home was always filled with flowers, a garden of remembrance is planned in her honor outside the palace gates where so many mourners laid floral tributes to Diana in the weeks following her death.

ACKNOWLEDGMENTS

State reception, Brisbane, Australia, April 1983

I would like to thank the following:
My husband, Alan, for putting up with endless interruption of our lives.
My father, Terry Fincher, for being the best teacher in this business and his endless advice and the use of some of his photographs.
Judy Wade for her constant friendship and professionalism.
Jim Brown for his expert advice and assistance.
Russel West for his technical help and use of one of his photographs.
The Marquessa de Varella for use of my last photographs of Diana.
Sally Drinkwater, my sister, for her endless help with the photographs.
Also my sister, Lucy Levenson, for use of some of her photographs from assignments that I could not cover.
My mother for nonstop tea during long working hours.
The editorial team at Callaway for all its hard work.
And finally all the people and press officers who have helped me over the years to travel the world.